Math Workbook for Kindergarteners

1000+ Practice Questions - Addition, Subtraction, and Counting | Homeschool Worksheets (Ages 4-6)

Mr. Patterson

Number Tracing

Follow the Arrows to Draw Each Number

1 1. ___

1. 2 2. 3. ___

1. 3 2. ___

1. 4 2. 3. ___

3. 1. 5 2. ___

1. 6 2. ___

1. 7 2. ___

1. 2. 8 3. ___

2. 1. 9 3. ___

1. 10 2. ___

Practice Drawing Numbers 1-10

1	1	1	1	1
2	2	2	2	2
3	3	3	3	3
4	4	4	4	4
5	5	5	5	5
6	6	6	6	6
7	7	7	7	7
8	8	8	8	8
9	9	9	9	9
10	10	10	10	10

Counting

Count and Circle the Correct Amount of Objects

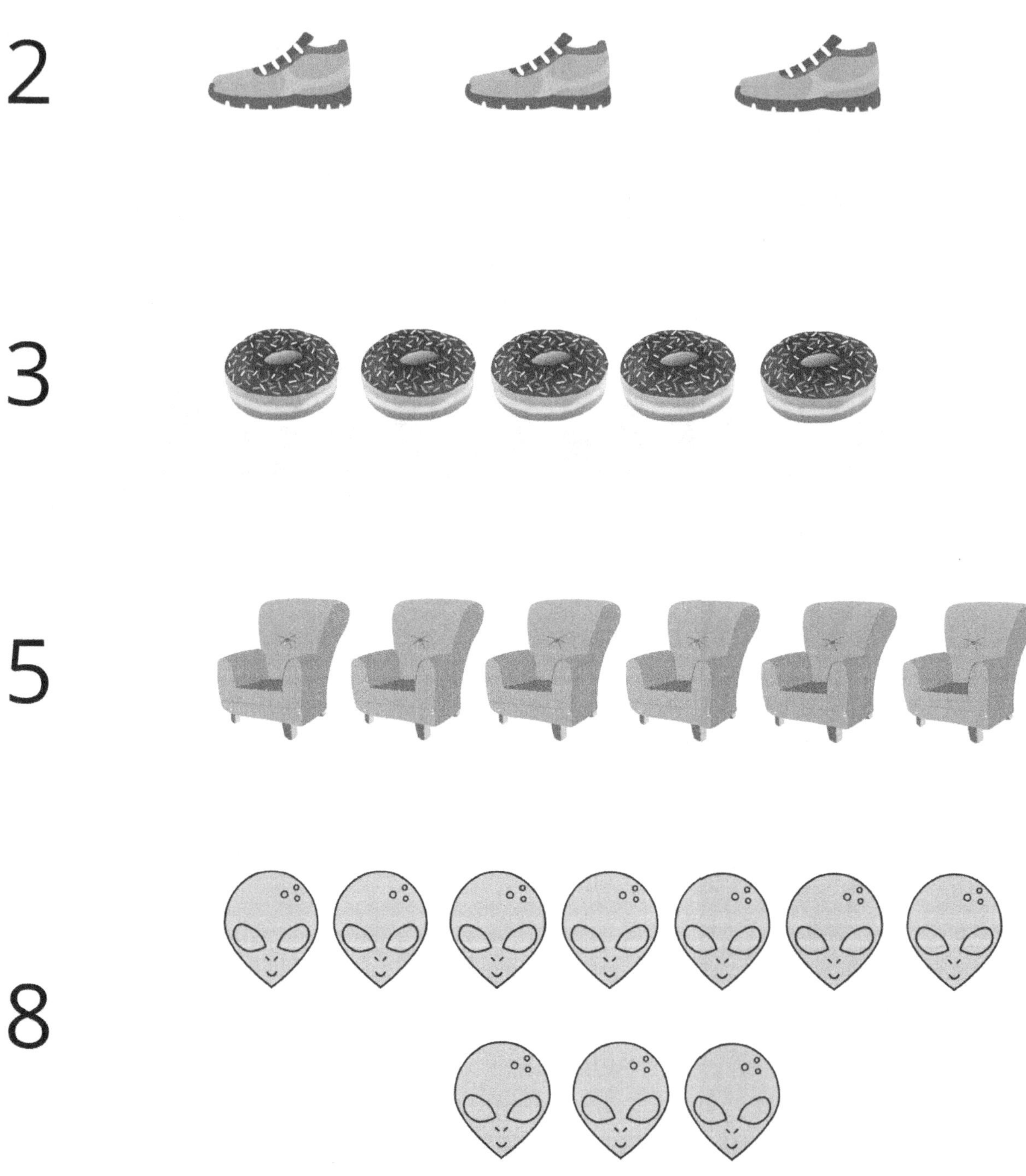

Count and Circle the Correct Amount of Objects

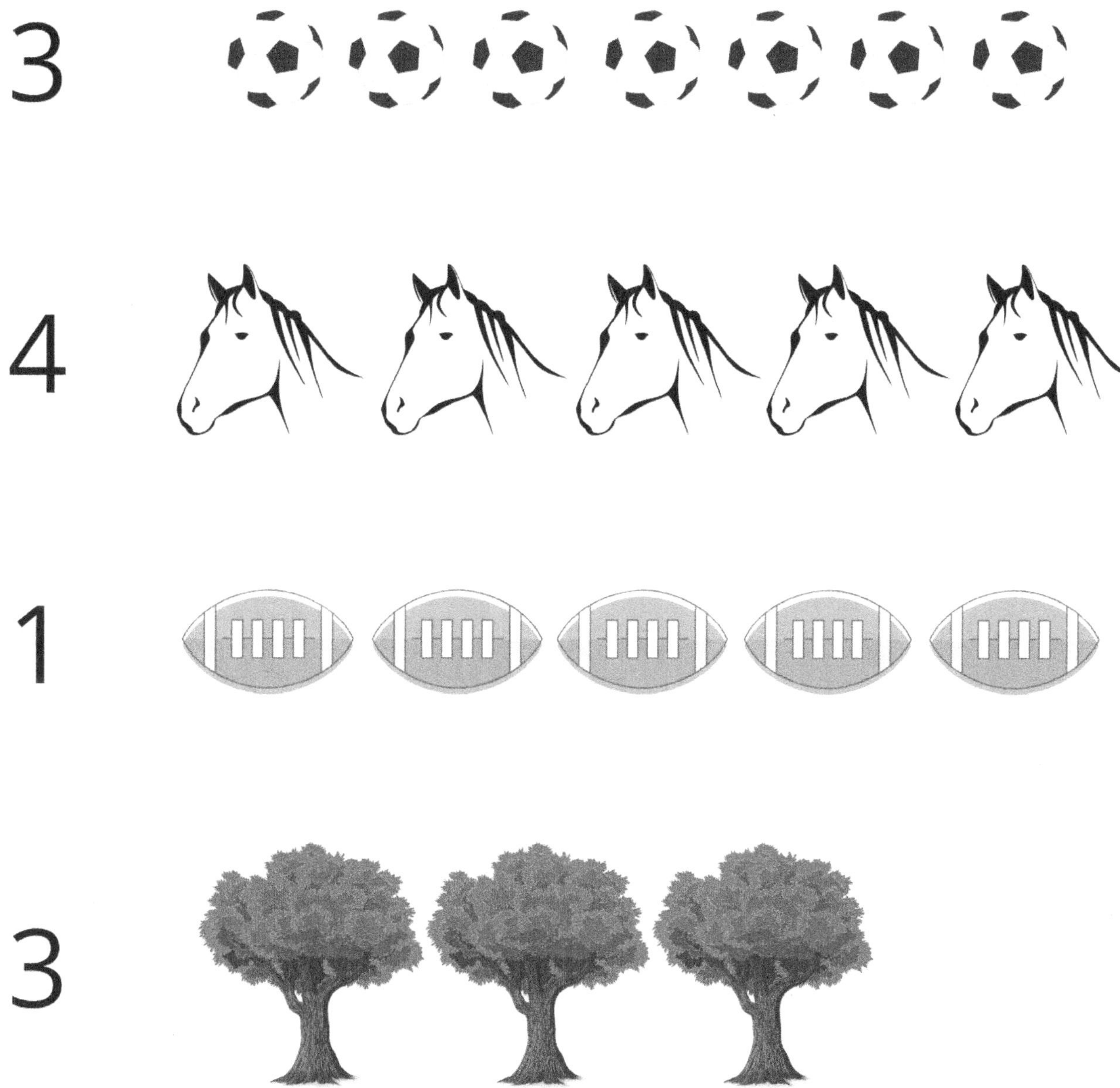

Count and Circle the Correct Amount of Objects

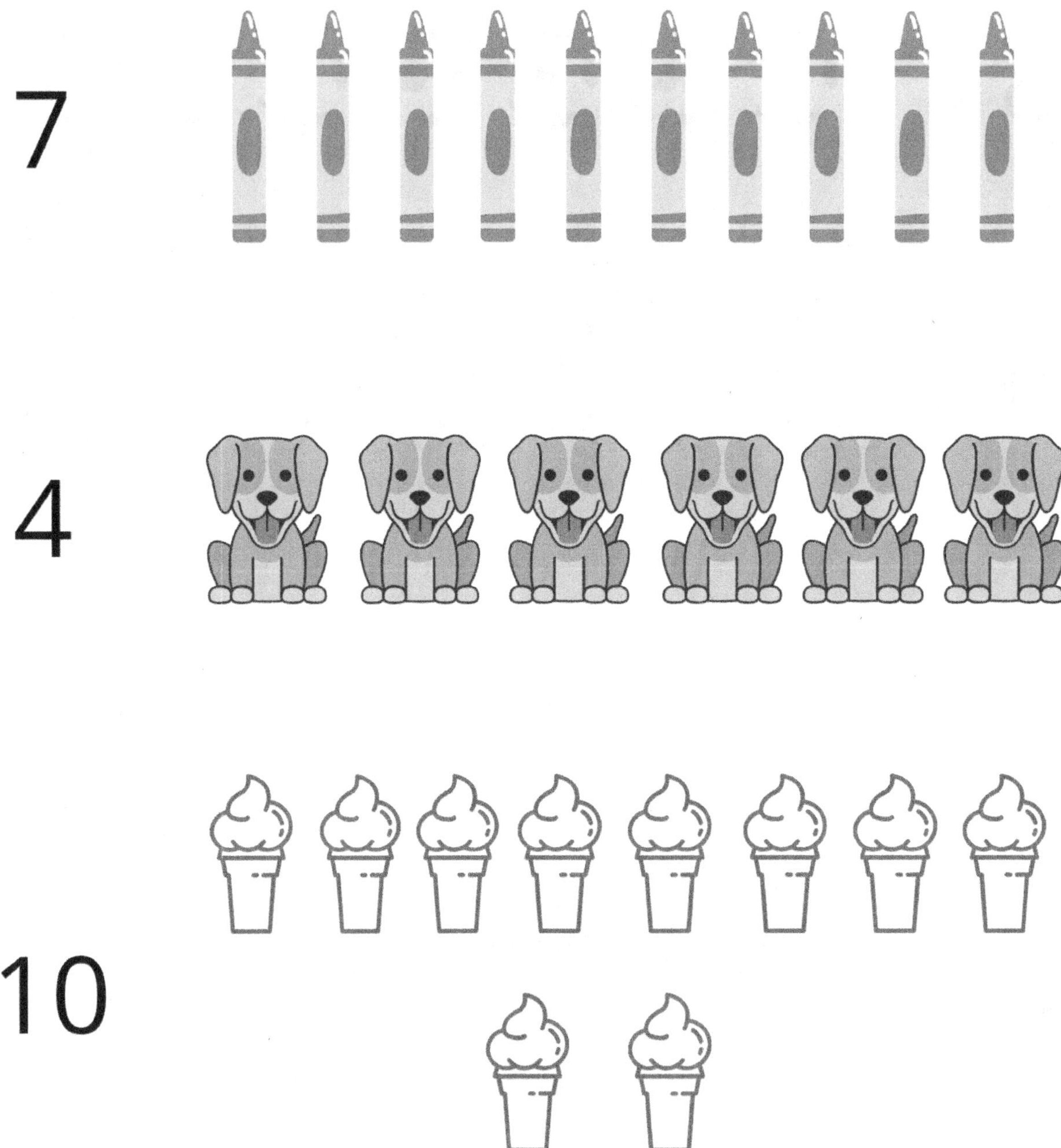

Count the number of corners on each shape

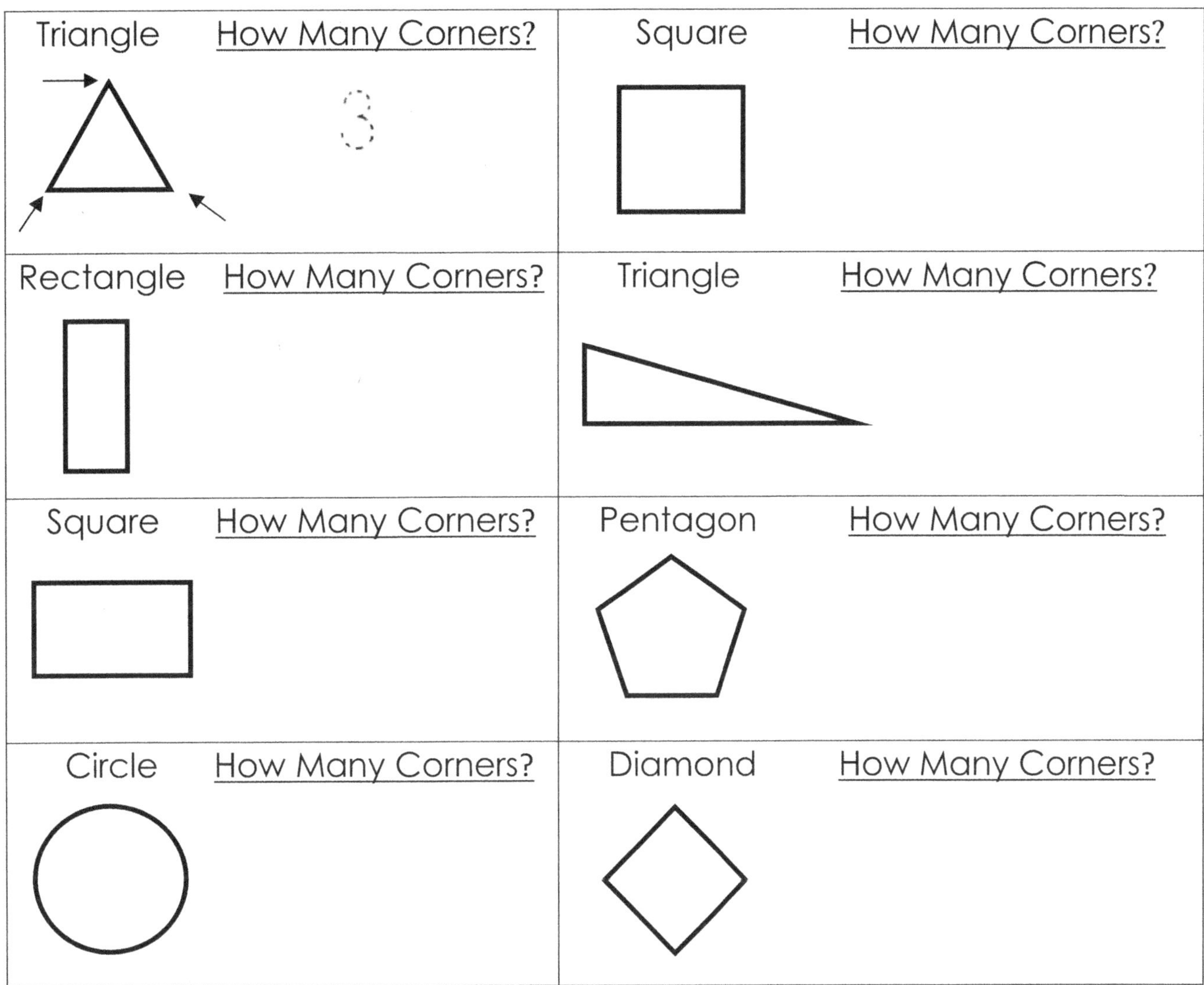

Count the animals and write in the box

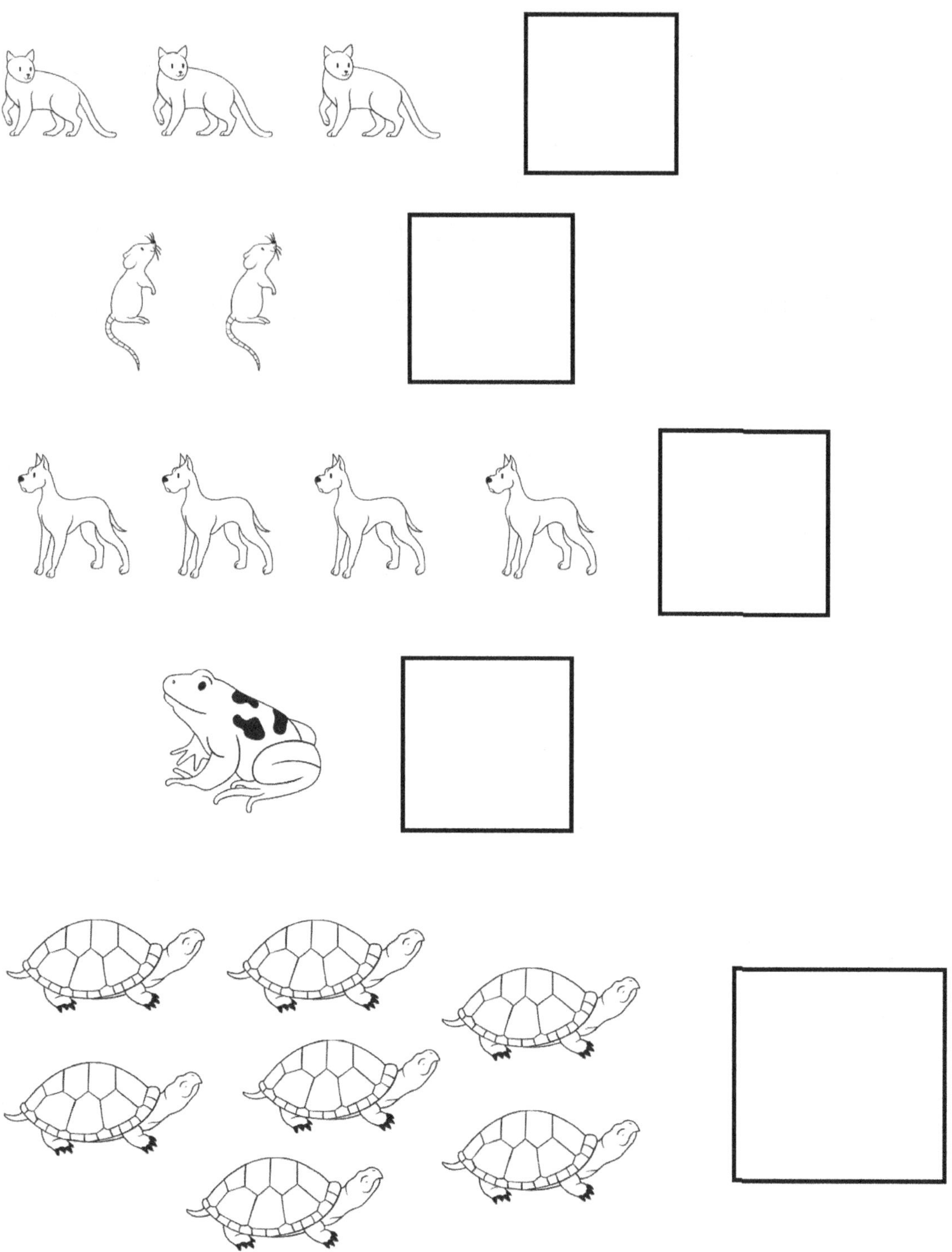

Count the animals of each type

+

+ ADDITION +

+

Count the Food, Write the Numbers, Find the Total!

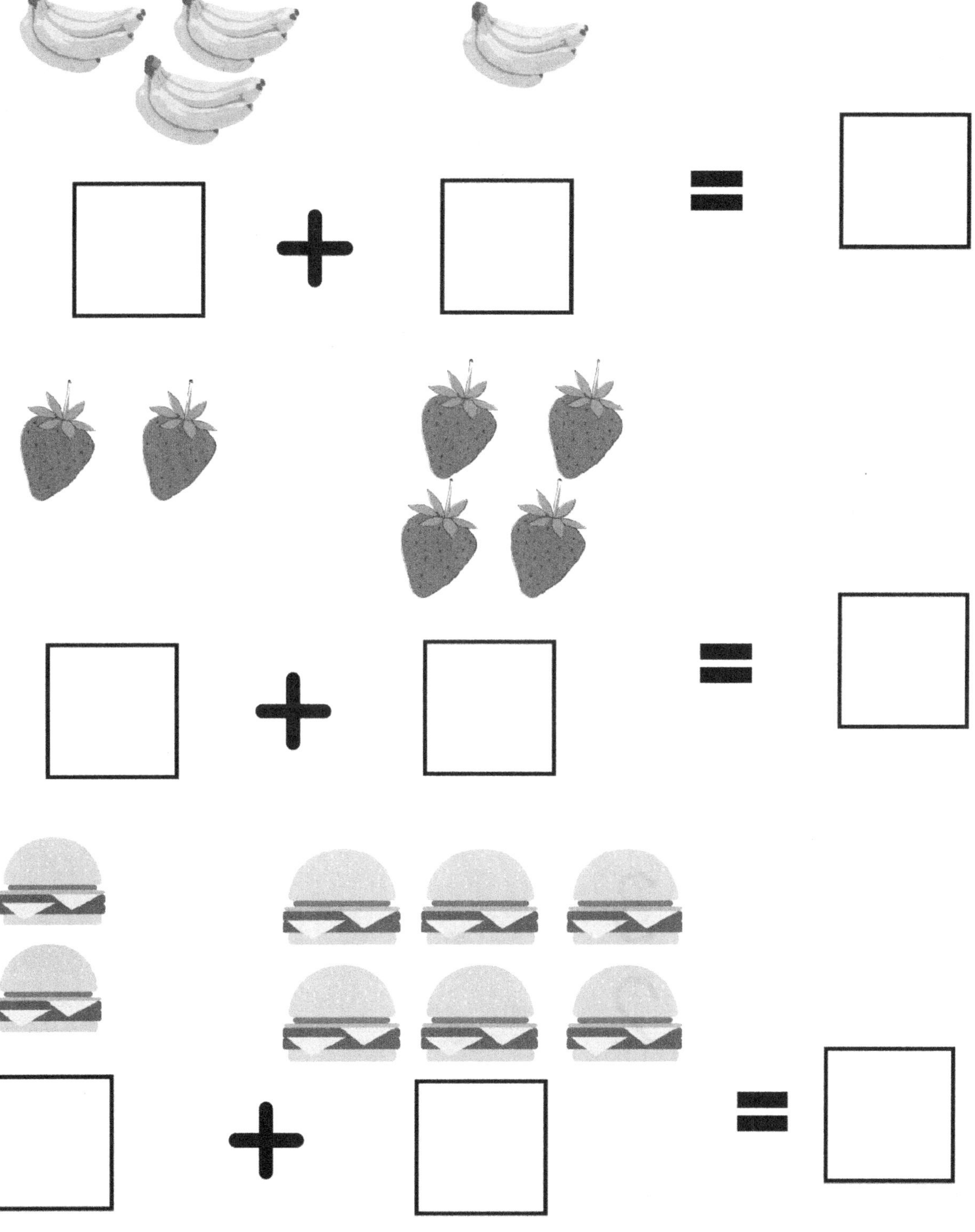

Addition (1–10)

$$\begin{array}{r} 3 \\ +\ 3 \\ \hline \end{array}$$

$$\begin{array}{r} 2 \\ +\ 5 \\ \hline \end{array}$$

$$\begin{array}{r} 5 \\ +\ 5 \\ \hline \end{array}$$

$$\begin{array}{r} 3 \\ +\ 2 \\ \hline \end{array}$$

Addition (1-10)

$$\begin{array}{r} 2 \\ +\ 2 \\ \hline \end{array}$$

$$\begin{array}{r} 1 \\ +\ 2 \\ \hline \end{array}$$

$$\begin{array}{r} 2 \\ +\ 6 \\ \hline \end{array}$$

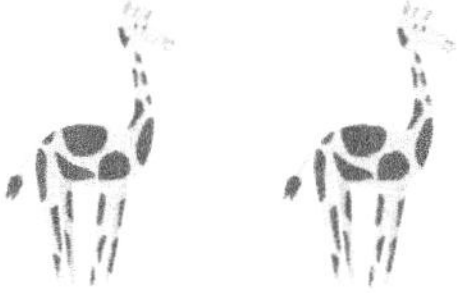

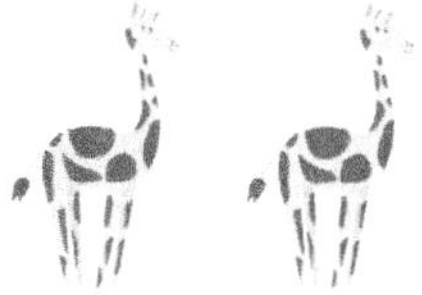

$$\begin{array}{r} 5 \\ +\ 2 \\ \hline \end{array}$$

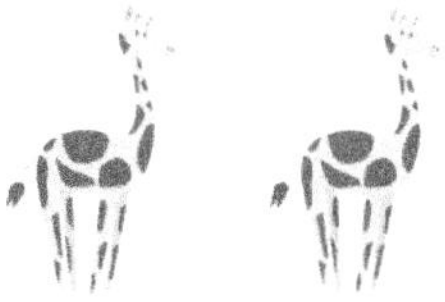

Addition (1-10)

4
+ 5
___

2
+ 1
___

3
+ 2
___

8
+ 1
___

Addition (1–10)

$$\begin{array}{r} 3 \\ +\ 1 \\ \hline \end{array}$$

$$\begin{array}{r} 1 \\ +\ 1 \\ \hline \end{array}$$

$$\begin{array}{r} 5 \\ +\ 5 \\ \hline \end{array}$$

$$\begin{array}{r} 2 \\ +\ 2 \\ \hline \end{array}$$

$$\begin{array}{r} 2 \\ +\ 1 \\ \hline \end{array}$$

Addition (1-10)

		Number line
4	+ 3	0 1 2 3 4 5 6 7 8 9 10 (jumps: 1, 2, 3)
= 7		

Problem	Number line
1 + 3 =	0 1 2 3 4 5 6 7 8 9 10
5 + 4 =	0 1 2 3 4 5 6 7 8 9 10
4 + 3 =	0 1 2 3 4 5 6 7 8 9 10
2 + 7 =	0 1 2 3 4 5 6 7 8 9 10
5 + 5 =	0 1 2 3 4 5 6 7 8 9 10
9 + 1 =	0 1 2 3 4 5 6 7 8 9 10
3 + 3 =	0 1 2 3 4 5 6 7 8 9 10

Addition (1-10)

2
+ 8

0 1 2 3 4 5 6 7 8 9 10

6
+ 1

0 1 2 3 4 5 6 7 8 9 10

1
+ 3

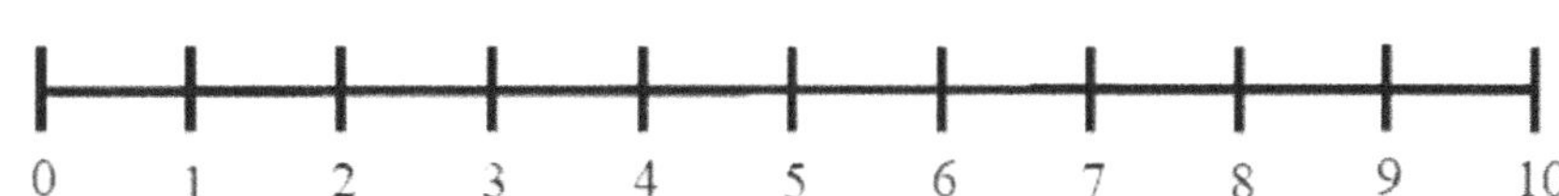

1
+ 5

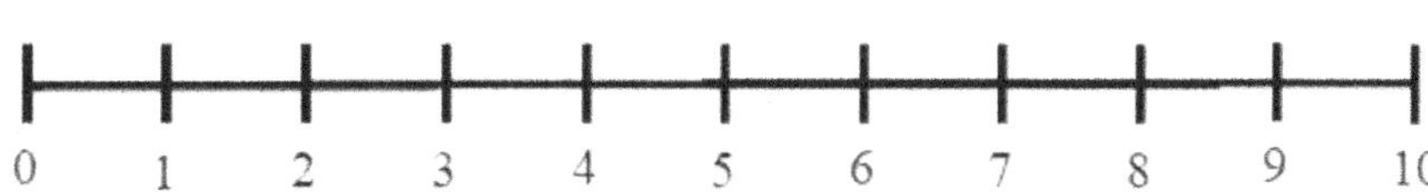

4
+ 4

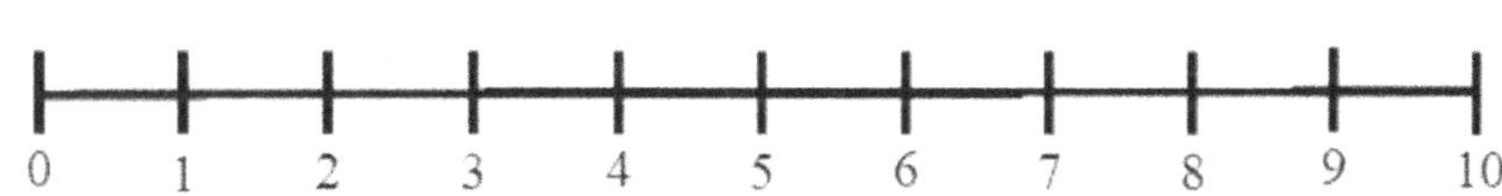

2
+ 2

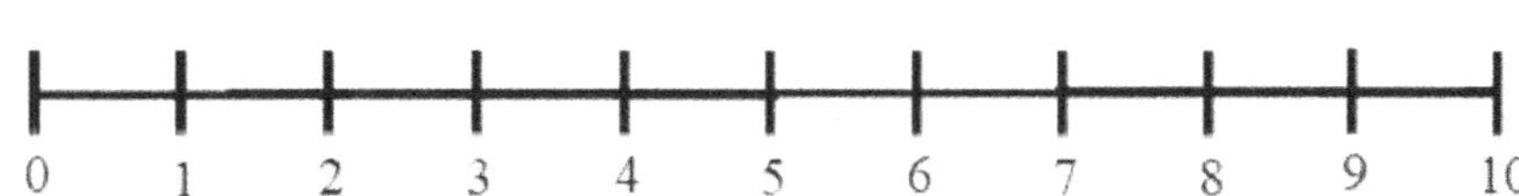

3
+ 4

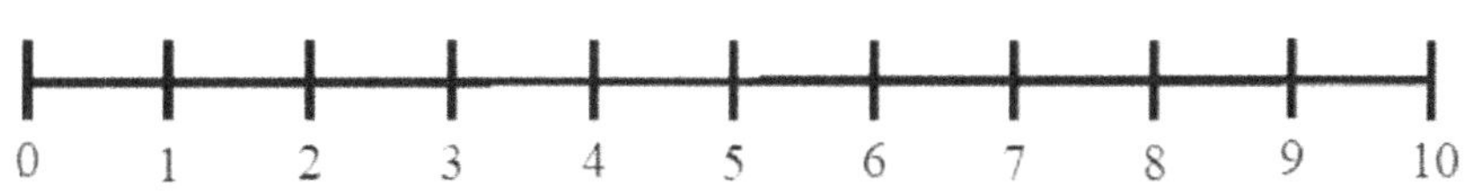

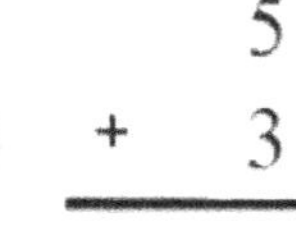

5
+ 3

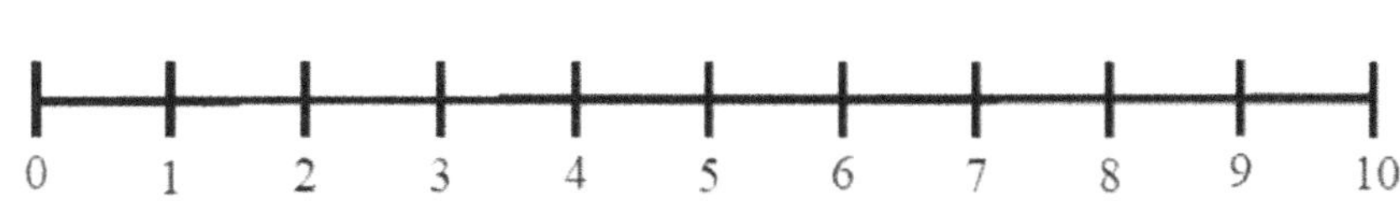

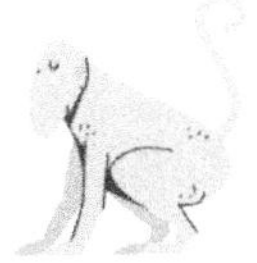

Addition (1-10)

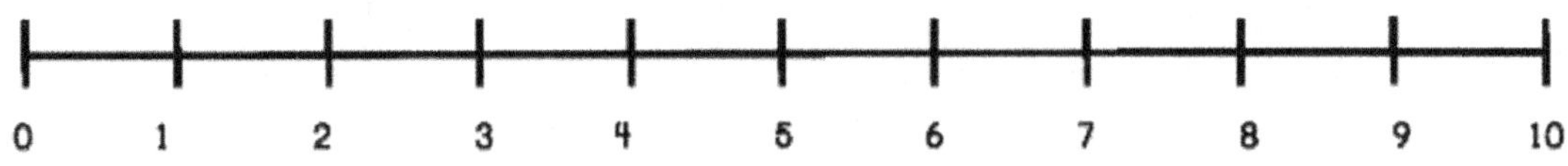

$$\begin{array}{r} 4 \\ +\ 3 \\ \hline \end{array} \qquad \begin{array}{r} 2 \\ +\ 5 \\ \hline \end{array} \qquad \begin{array}{r} 4 \\ +\ 6 \\ \hline \end{array}$$

$$\begin{array}{r} 2 \\ +\ 2 \\ \hline \end{array} \qquad \begin{array}{r} 3 \\ +\ 1 \\ \hline \end{array} \qquad \begin{array}{r} 2 \\ +\ 6 \\ \hline \end{array}$$

$$\begin{array}{r} 5 \\ +\ 2 \\ \hline \end{array} \qquad \begin{array}{r} 1 \\ +\ 4 \\ \hline \end{array} \qquad \begin{array}{r} 2 \\ +\ 7 \\ \hline \end{array}$$

$$\begin{array}{r} 3 \\ +\ 6 \\ \hline \end{array} \qquad \begin{array}{r} 4 \\ +\ 4 \\ \hline \end{array} \qquad \begin{array}{r} 5 \\ +\ 3 \\ \hline \end{array}$$

$$\begin{array}{r} 2 \\ +\ 8 \\ \hline \end{array} \qquad \begin{array}{r} 5 \\ +\ 1 \\ \hline \end{array} \qquad \begin{array}{r} 1 \\ +\ 9 \\ \hline \end{array}$$

Addition (1-10)

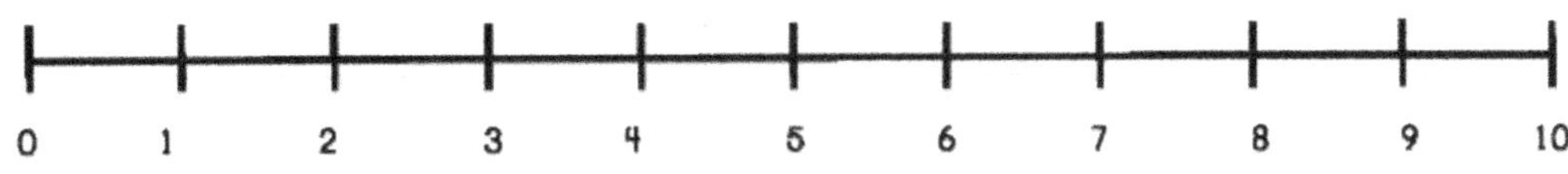

3 + 3	5 + 5	4 + 1
2 + 3	5 + 1	2 + 1
8 + 2	1 + 9	2 + 7
3 + 7	4 + 3	2 + 3
2 + 6	5 + 5	1 + 6

Addition (1-10)

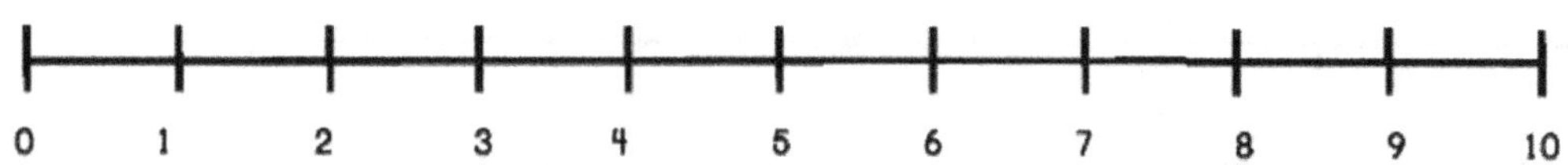

7 + 3	2 + 1	2 + 6
4 + 2	5 + 1	2 + 8
6 + 2	1 + 6	3 + 7
3 + 2	4 + 4	5 + 3
2 + 8	5 + 1	1 + 3

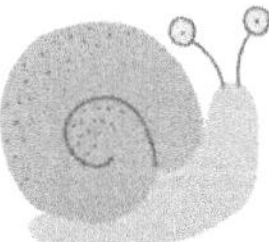

Addition 1–10

(a+b = b+a)

2 + 5 =
5 + 2 =

3 + 4 =
4 + 3 =

9 + 1 =
1 + 9 =

7 + 2 =
2 + 7 =

8 + 1 =
1 + 8 =

Addition 1-10

(a+b = b+a)

4 + 2 =

2 + 4 =

3 + 6 =

6 + 3 =

2 + 3 =

3 + 2 =

7 + 1 =

1 + 7 =

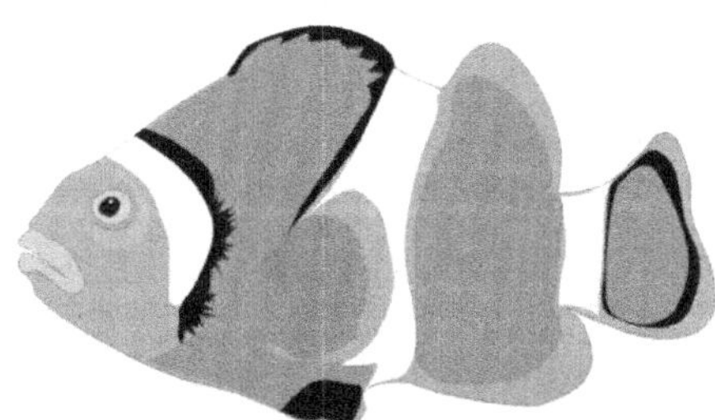

5 + 1 =

1 + 5 =

- SUBTRACTION -

Subtraction (1-10)

Cross Out the Bananas to Find the Answer

5 - 3 ___	8 - 4 ___
4 - 2 ___	6 - 4 ___
4 - 1 ___	7 - 5 ___
7 - 7 ___	7 - 2 ___

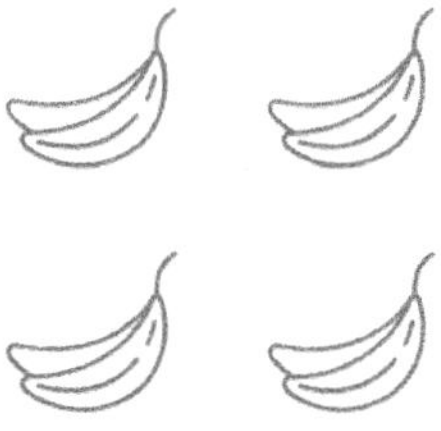

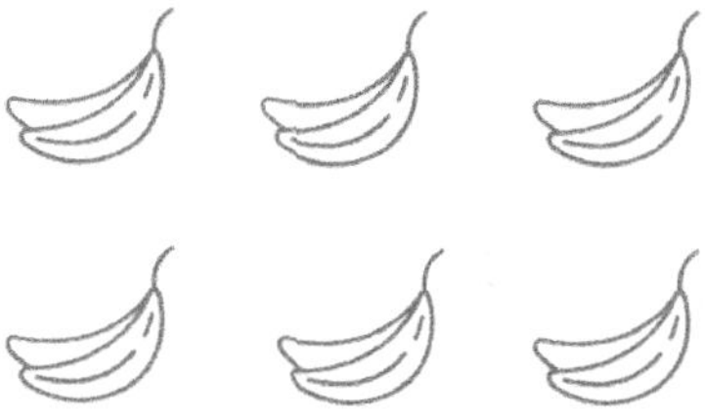

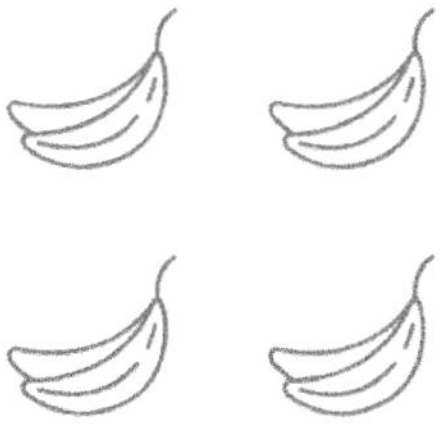

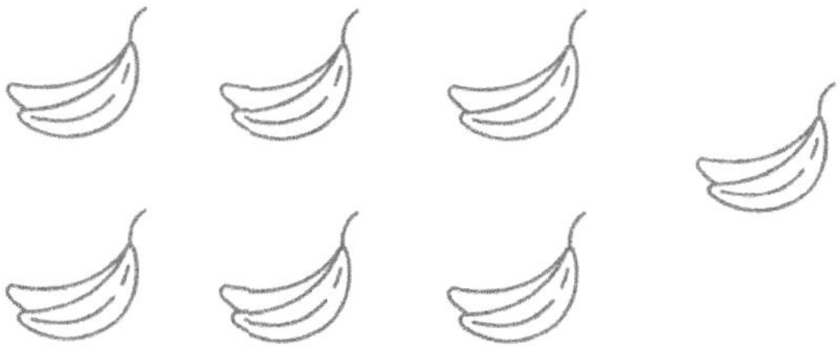

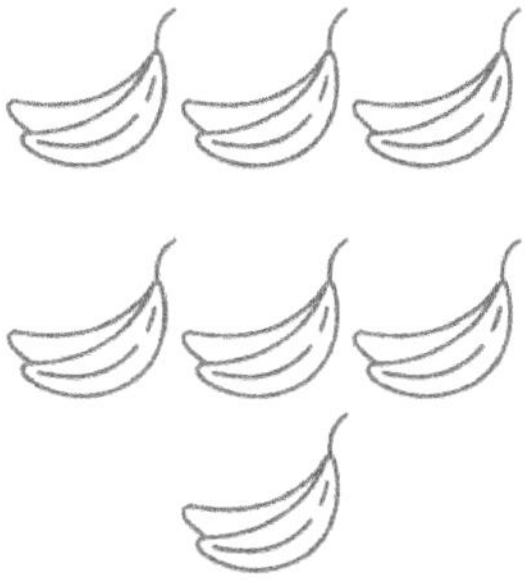

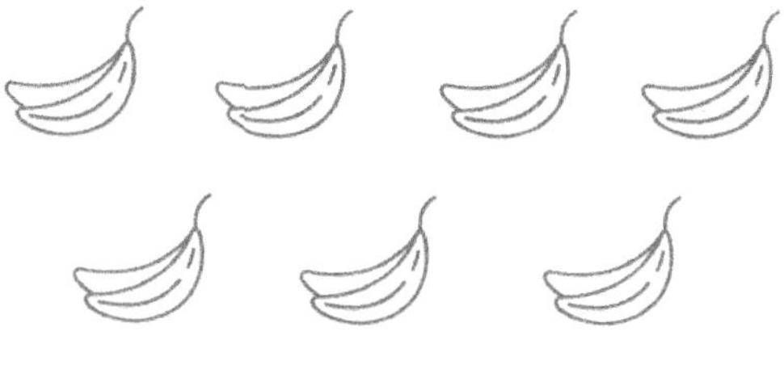

Subtraction (1-10)

Cross Out the Cats to Find the Answer

$$\begin{array}{r} 5 \\ -\ 2 \\ \hline \end{array}$$

$$\begin{array}{r} 6 \\ -\ 0 \\ \hline \end{array}$$

$$\begin{array}{r} 9 \\ -\ 6 \\ \hline \end{array}$$

$$\begin{array}{r} 9 \\ -\ 2 \\ \hline \end{array}$$

$$\begin{array}{r} 8 \\ -\ 7 \\ \hline \end{array}$$

$$\begin{array}{r} 9 \\ -\ 5 \\ \hline \end{array}$$

$$\begin{array}{r} 2 \\ -\ 2 \\ \hline \end{array}$$

$$\begin{array}{r} 4 \\ -\ 3 \\ \hline \end{array}$$

Subtraction (1-10)

Cross Out the Turtles to Find the Answer

8	5
- 3	- 4

6	9
- 2	- 7

8	7
- 5	- 4

8	5
- 8	- 2

Subtraction (1-10)

Cross Out the Birds to Find the Answer

6
- 4
____

9
- 2
____

8
- 4
____

5
- 2
____

8
- 2
____

4
- 1
____

9
- 5
____

8
- 5
____

Subtraction (1-10)

Use the Number Line to Subtract

7
\- 3
___
4

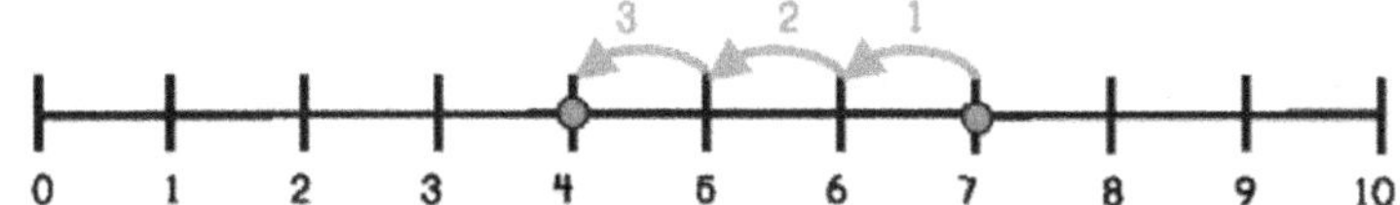

8
\- 4
___

0 1 2 3 4 5 6 7 8 9 10

4
\- 4
___

0 1 2 3 4 5 6 7 8 9 10

6
\- 1
___

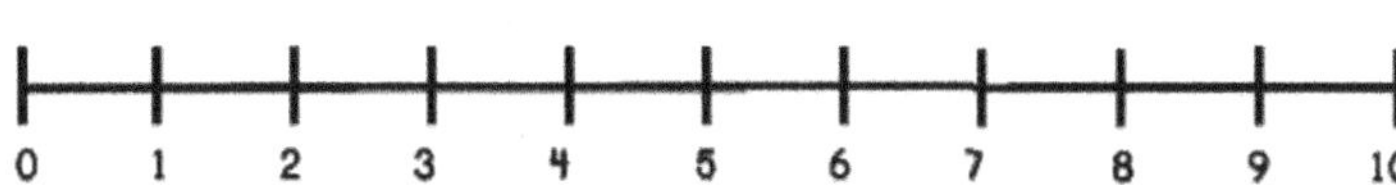

8
\- 7
___

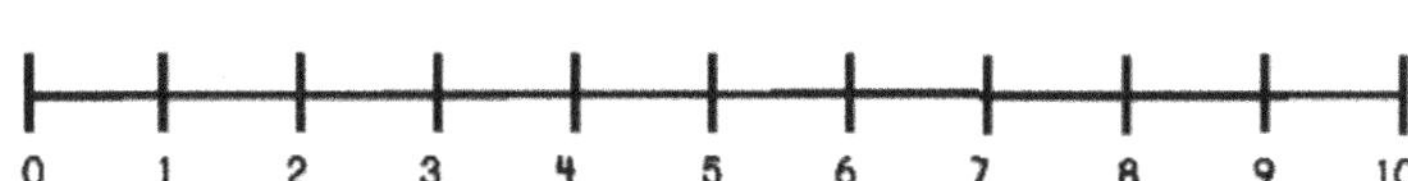

9
\- 5
___

0 1 2 3 4 5 6 7 8 9 10

7
\- 4
___

0 1 2 3 4 5 6 7 8 9 10

10
\- 6
___

0 1 2 3 4 5 6 7 8 9 10

Subtraction (1-10)

Use the Number Line to Subtract

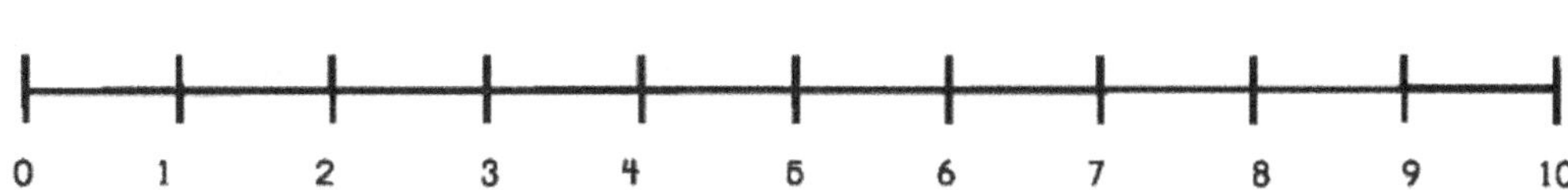

4 - 2	9 - 4	7 - 1
8 - 4	6 - 2	7 - 4
5 - 3	4 - 1	6 - 6
10 - 3	3 - 0	6 - 4

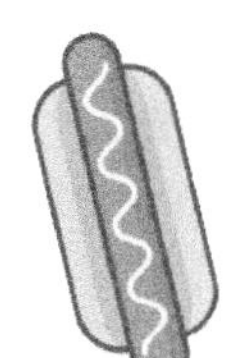

Subtraction (1-10)

Use the Number Line to Subtract

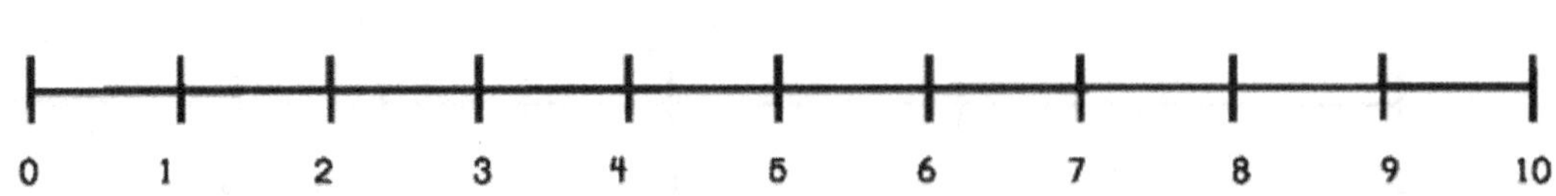

9 - 3	5 - 4	8 - 6
7 - 2	4 - 1	9 - 5
6 - 3	9 - 7	7 - 5
8 - 1	9 - 4	8 - 4

Subtraction (1-10)

Use the Number Line to Subtract

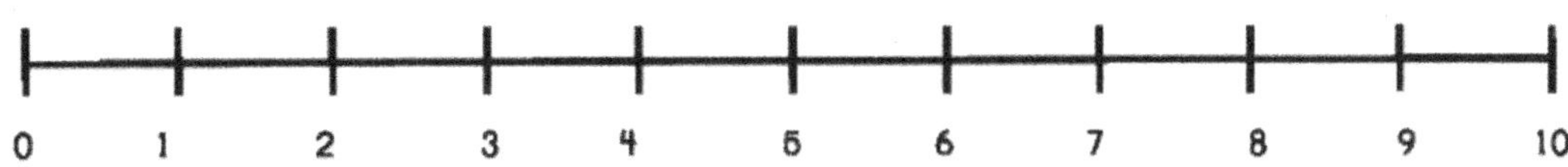

5 - 2	6 - 3	8 - 5
7 - 7	5 - 1	8 - 3
5 - 3	6 - 4	9 - 5
6 - 6	9 - 2	10 - 7

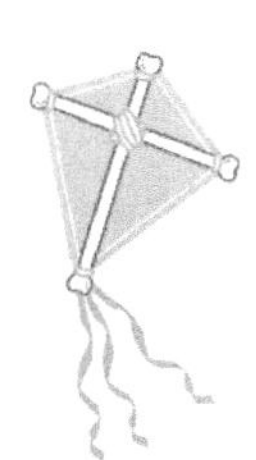

Subtraction (1-10)

Use the Number Line to Subtract

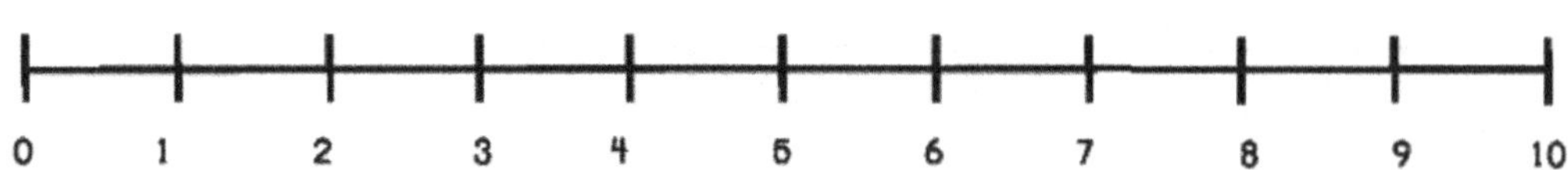

9 - 5	6 - 0	7 - 2
8 - 5	9 - 7	6 - 3
7 - 4	8 - 3	4 - 2
6 - 1	8 - 6	9 - 3

Subtraction (1-10)

Use the Number Line to Subtract

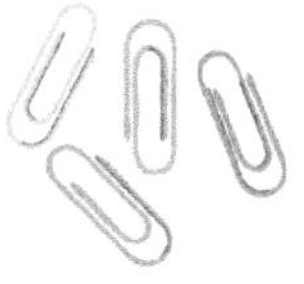

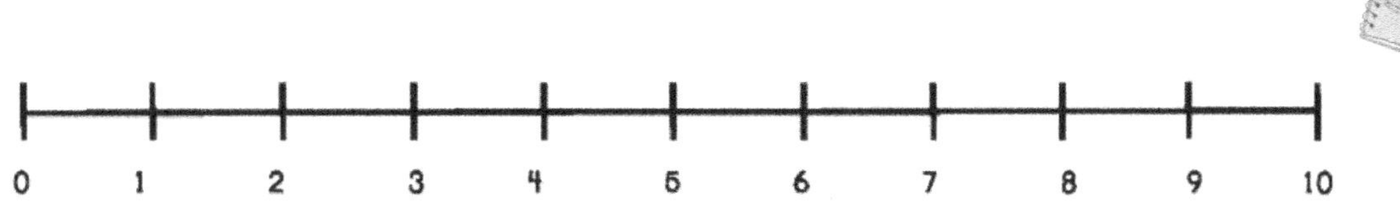

10 - 5	9 - 5	5 - 3
6 - 2	8 - 5	7 - 2
9 - 8	8 - 1	6 - 4
7 - 5	9 - 2	6 - 0

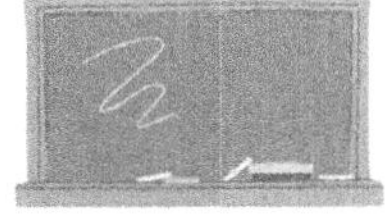

Addition and Subtraction Practice Questions

Answer Key for This Section Included at End of Book

A

2 + 4 = _	4 + 2 = _	7 + 2 = _	6 + 3 = _	4 + 1 = _
5 + 3 = _	5 + 2 = _	2 + 1 = _	3 + 4 = _	2 + 7 = _
5 + 4 = _	2 + 5 = _	5 + 2 = _	1 + 4 = _	4 + 5 = _
1 + 4 = _	7 + 2 = _	2 + 5 = _	3 + 2 = _	2 + 7 = _
5 + 3 = _	3 + 6 = _	5 + 1 = _	7 + 3 = __	4 + 2 = _
3 + 7 = __	1 + 9 = __	3 + 2 = _	2 + 5 = _	4 + 5 = _
2 + 7 = _	2 + 3 = _	4 + 5 = _	3 + 7 = __	1 + 5 = _
4 + 3 = _	2 + 4 = _	4 + 2 = _	1 + 8 = _	8 + 2 = __

B

8 + 2 = __	7 + 3 = __	3 + 3 = _	7 + 3 = __	5 + 5 = __
2 + 6 = _	2 + 8 = __	1 + 2 = _	8 + 2 = __	5 + 5 = __
6 + 1 = _	3 + 2 = _	5 + 4 = _	3 + 3 = _	3 + 3 = _
4 + 3 = _	4 + 5 = _	3 + 3 = _	7 + 1 = _	6 + 4 = __
2 + 7 = _	4 + 2 = _	5 + 5 = __	8 + 2 = __	5 + 2 = _
1 + 8 = _	2 + 6 = _	1 + 1 = _	2 + 2 = _	5 + 5 = __
2 + 7 = _	5 + 3 = _	7 + 3 = __	8 + 1 = _	1 + 7 = _
5 + 2 = _	3 + 7 = __	2 + 5 = _	3 + 4 = _	2 + 4 = _

C

2 + 3 = _	4 + 6 = __	3 + 3 = _	2 + 5 = _	2 + 5 = _
2 + 2 = _	5 + 4 = _	3 + 3 = _	1 + 3 = _	3 + 4 = _
1 + 3 = _	2 + 3 = _	3 + 6 = _	3 + 2 = _	3 + 7 = __
3 + 6 = _	8 + 1 = _	4 + 3 = _	6 + 2 = _	9 + 1 = __
4 + 4 = _	5 + 4 = _	1 + 9 = __	3 + 4 = _	4 + 2 = _
3 + 6 = _	7 + 2 = _	1 + 8 = _	7 + 1 = _	9 + 1 = __
4 + 2 = _	2 + 6 = _	2 + 3 = _	2 + 7 = _	1 + 3 = _
5 + 4 = _	4 + 3 = _	2 + 1 = _	3 + 6 = _	2 + 7 = _

D

3 + 2 = _	7 + 2 = _	2 + 2 = _	4 + 3 = _	2 + 8 = __
6 + 4 = __	2 + 6 = _	5 + 3 = _	4 + 3 = _	4 + 6 = __
8 + 2 = __	2 + 3 = _	2 + 3 = _	7 + 3 = __	3 + 7 = __
4 + 4 = _	1 + 7 = _	1 + 2 = _	3 + 3 = _	1 + 5 = _
1 + 7 = _	2 + 5 = _	7 + 3 = __	2 + 5 = _	9 + 1 = __
2 + 3 = _	2 + 6 = _	2 + 2 = _	3 + 4 = _	6 + 3 = _
7 + 1 = _	5 + 4 = _	3 + 5 = _	9 + 1 = __	6 + 2 = _
1 + 2 = _	1 + 5 = _	2 + 8 = __	4 + 1 = _	3 + 5 = _

E

4 + 3 = _	3 + 4 = _	2 + 5 = _	5 + 5 = __	6 + 2 = _
6 + 4 = __	1 + 1 = _	4 + 2 = _	7 + 2 = _	2 + 2 = _
3 + 5 = _	6 + 3 = _	1 + 5 = _	6 + 4 = __	5 + 2 = _
4 + 5 = _	3 + 4 = _	2 + 8 = __	6 + 3 = _	3 + 6 = _
2 + 4 = _	7 + 2 = _	7 + 1 = _	1 + 2 = _	1 + 8 = _
3 + 6 = _	2 + 6 = _	5 + 3 = _	6 + 4 = __	2 + 7 = _
3 + 3 = _	3 + 3 = _	7 + 2 = _	2 + 3 = _	3 + 6 = _
2 + 8 = __	3 + 7 = __	1 + 2 = _	3 + 7 = __	2 + 2 = _

F

2 + 8 = __	3 + 7 = __	5 + 3 = _	2 + 5 = _	6 + 2 = _
4 + 2 = _	1 + 8 = _	2 + 6 = _	1 + 4 = _	3 + 5 = _
1 + 4 = _	2 + 5 = _	3 + 2 = _	3 + 5 = _	7 + 3 = __
2 + 3 = _	7 + 2 = _	5 + 3 = _	1 + 5 = _	2 + 8 = __
2 + 3 = _	3 + 2 = _	4 + 4 = _	4 + 5 = _	5 + 1 = _
5 + 5 = __	6 + 4 = __	5 + 2 = _	5 + 4 = _	3 + 6 = _
2 + 1 = _	5 + 5 = __	6 + 4 = __	2 + 8 = __	3 + 5 = _
3 + 6 = _	6 + 1 = _	6 + 2 = _	8 + 2 = __	4 + 1 = _

G

5 + 2 = _	8 + 1 = _	2 + 5 = _	1 + 9 = __	4 + 3 = _
2 + 3 = _	4 + 2 = _	4 + 5 = _	3 + 5 = _	7 + 2 = _
3 + 7 = __	3 + 7 = __	1 + 9 = __	6 + 2 = _	4 + 4 = _
3 + 7 = __	8 + 2 = __	3 + 4 = _	6 + 3 = _	7 + 1 = _
2 + 6 = _	2 + 5 = _	4 + 3 = _	3 + 7 = __	2 + 6 = _
4 + 6 = __	3 + 6 = _	5 + 4 = _	6 + 2 = _	3 + 1 = _
4 + 6 = __	5 + 1 = _	4 + 6 = __	7 + 1 = _	4 + 6 = __
4 + 1 = _	4 + 1 = _	7 + 2 = _	5 + 2 = _	2 + 8 = __

H

9 + 1 = ___	5 + 5 = ___	4 + 4 = _	8 + 2 = ___	1 + 9 = ___
5 + 5 = ___	1 + 7 = _	6 + 2 = _	3 + 7 = ___	2 + 3 = _
2 + 6 = _	3 + 3 = _	2 + 4 = _	3 + 3 = _	1 + 5 = _
2 + 6 = _	5 + 3 = _	1 + 9 = ___	1 + 8 = _	3 + 7 = ___
3 + 7 = ___	7 + 2 = _	4 + 1 = _	2 + 7 = _	6 + 3 = _
2 + 1 = _	6 + 2 = _	5 + 5 = ___	4 + 3 = _	3 + 5 = _
1 + 8 = _	4 + 3 = _	4 + 3 = _	5 + 5 = ___	1 + 8 = _
2 + 8 = ___	7 + 2 = _	4 + 1 = _	6 + 2 = _	6 + 3 = _

I

3 + 6 = _	7 + 1 = _	1 + 9 = __	2 + 4 = _	6 + 4 = __
5 + 3 = _	7 + 3 = __	6 + 2 = _	3 + 5 = _	6 + 4 = __
1 + 8 = _	4 + 1 = _	2 + 3 = _	6 + 3 = _	8 + 1 = _
3 + 7 = __	4 + 2 = _	3 + 5 = _	6 + 4 = __	2 + 3 = _
8 + 1 = _	4 + 5 = _	6 + 2 = _	1 + 4 = _	3 + 7 = __
6 + 4 = __	4 + 4 = _	9 + 1 = __	7 + 2 = _	5 + 2 = _
3 + 7 = __	3 + 6 = _	3 + 7 = __	3 + 7 = __	2 + 3 = _
2 + 2 = _	1 + 3 = _	4 + 3 = _	7 + 2 = _	2 + 1 = _

J

3 + 6 = _	8 + 2 = __	5 + 4 = _	1 + 2 = _	3 + 1 = _
4 + 2 = _	3 + 3 = _	4 + 4 = _	3 + 1 = _	1 + 2 = _
3 + 7 = __	3 + 3 = _	3 + 4 = _	2 + 4 = _	7 + 3 = __
1 + 9 = __	1 + 1 = _	1 + 4 = _	5 + 4 = _	3 + 1 = _
8 + 2 = __	5 + 4 = _	1 + 5 = _	1 + 4 = _	2 + 6 = _
5 + 2 = _	6 + 1 = _	3 + 7 = __	1 + 3 = _	1 + 4 = _
4 + 3 = _	6 + 3 = _	4 + 4 = _	4 + 5 = _	3 + 4 = _
2 + 4 = _	2 + 5 = _	6 + 3 = _	1 + 3 = _	5 + 3 = _

K

1 + 9 = __	2 + 3 = _	5 + 4 = _	2 + 1 = _	8 + 2 = __
2 + 4 = _	2 + 8 = __	6 + 3 = _	2 + 6 = _	7 + 2 = _
6 + 2 = _	2 + 8 = __	2 + 2 = _	2 + 8 = __	6 + 3 = _
2 + 4 = _	3 + 2 = _	2 + 5 = _	8 + 2 = __	2 + 3 = _
1 + 3 = _	6 + 2 = _	2 + 6 = _	1 + 3 = _	3 + 2 = _
5 + 2 = _	3 + 3 = _	1 + 3 = _	2 + 7 = _	3 + 7 = __
6 + 2 = _	2 + 1 = _	4 + 1 = _	3 + 6 = _	3 + 7 = __
4 + 2 = _	9 + 1 = __	5 + 3 = _	3 + 4 = _	1 + 9 = __

L

5 - 5 = _	10 - 6 = _	8 - 1 = _	5 - 5 = _	7 - 7 = _
8 - 4 = _	7 - 6 = _	10 - 9 = _	5 - 2 = _	9 - 9 = _
8 - 4 = _	7 - 3 = _	9 - 7 = _	6 - 4 = _	6 - 6 = _
7 - 5 = _	8 - 2 = _	9 - 3 = _	6 - 4 = _	3 - 2 = _
8 - 7 = _	9 - 8 = _	7 - 2 = _	5 - 3 = _	6 - 5 = _
8 - 5 = _	8 - 2 = _	8 - 4 = _	3 - 3 = _	9 - 6 = _
9 - 8 = _	9 - 3 = _	9 - 8 = _	10 - 4 = _	7 - 6 = _
9 - 6 = _	8 - 6 = _	8 - 8 = _	8 - 7 = _	9 - 3 = _

M

8 - 7 = _	4 - 1 = _	9 - 1 = _	9 - 6 = _	9 - 2 = _
6 - 1 = _	8 - 7 = _	9 - 6 = _	8 - 4 = _	8 - 3 = _
9 - 8 = _	8 - 3 = _	10 - 1 = _	8 - 5 = _	6 - 2 = _
9 - 1 = _	5 - 3 = _	10 - 8 = _	7 - 3 = _	7 - 6 = _
9 - 2 = _	4 - 2 = _	9 - 7 = _	8 - 5 = _	9 - 5 = _
8 - 8 = _	6 - 4 = _	4 - 2 = _	2 - 2 = _	3 - 2 = _
10 - 1 = _	7 - 3 = _	9 - 5 = _	9 - 1 = _	3 - 2 = _
4 - 3 = _	6 - 6 = _	6 - 2 = _	9 - 2 = _	9 - 6 = _

N

9 - 6 = _	5 - 2 = _	8 - 4 = _	4 - 4 = _	3 - 2 = _
10 - 4 = _	9 - 4 = _	8 - 4 = _	6 - 1 = _	6 - 5 = _
9 - 4 = _	5 - 1 = _	10 - 9 = _	2 - 2 = _	7 - 1 = _
10 - 8 = _	8 - 5 = _	9 - 4 = _	6 - 1 = _	10 - 9 = _
4 - 4 = _	6 - 6 = _	10 - 3 = _	1 - 1 = _	8 - 6 = _
8 - 3 = _	6 - 5 = _	7 - 3 = _	7 - 3 = _	7 - 7 = _
4 - 2 = _	4 - 3 = _	9 - 4 = _	7 - 2 = _	8 - 7 = _
10 - 7 = _	9 - 2 = _	5 - 3 = _	2 - 1 = _	10 - 8 = _

O

6 - 4 = _	2 - 1 = _	5 - 3 = _	6 - 2 = _	10 - 8 = _
6 - 5 = _	9 - 2 = _	6 - 3 = _	6 - 5 = _	5 - 4 = _
9 - 5 = _	8 - 5 = _	4 - 2 = _	2 - 2 = _	6 - 1 = _
6 - 4 = _	9 - 9 = _	6 - 2 = _	10 - 2 = _	9 - 1 = _
3 - 2 = _	8 - 4 = _	10 - 4 = _	10 - 4 = _	8 - 5 = _
5 - 2 = _	4 - 3 = _	9 - 7 = _	3 - 2 = _	5 - 3 = _
6 - 5 = _	8 - 4 = _	8 - 3 = _	8 - 7 = _	4 - 3 = _
8 - 6 = _	8 - 2 = _	8 - 3 = _	5 - 3 = _	8 - 5 = _

P

5 - 5 = _	6 - 4 = _	10 - 8 = _	4 - 4 = _	9 - 5 = _
10 - 5 = _	3 - 2 = _	8 - 4 = _	6 - 4 = _	9 - 2 = _
4 - 4 = _	6 - 5 = _	7 - 3 = _	5 - 4 = _	1 - 1 = _
5 - 4 = _	5 - 5 = _	8 - 1 = _	4 - 2 = _	9 - 7 = _
7 - 4 = _	4 - 1 = _	8 - 5 = _	9 - 6 = _	9 - 3 = _
9 - 8 = _	6 - 5 = _	8 - 5 = _	7 - 4 = _	8 - 3 = _
9 - 1 = _	7 - 3 = _	9 - 8 = _	9 - 2 = _	2 - 1 = _
9 - 1 = _	9 - 8 = _	9 - 4 = _	9 - 5 = _	8 - 4 = _

Q

8 - 3 = _	5 - 5 = _	4 - 2 = _	9 - 9 = _	6 - 2 = _
9 - 4 = _	8 - 3 = _	9 - 6 = _	6 - 2 = _	6 - 2 = _
6 - 5 = _	7 - 1 = _	7 - 5 = _	4 - 3 = _	5 - 1 = _
6 - 5 = _	7 - 3 = _	9 - 7 = _	10 - 6 = _	8 - 4 = _
2 - 1 = _	9 - 4 = _	5 - 5 = _	5 - 3 = _	7 - 5 = _
6 - 3 = _	9 - 3 = _	5 - 1 = _	8 - 2 = _	6 - 3 = _
7 - 2 = _	10 - 9 = _	8 - 4 = _	7 - 6 = _	4 - 3 = _
6 - 4 = _	9 - 2 = _	6 - 6 = _	9 - 2 = _	6 - 5 = _

R

8 - 2 = _	7 - 4 = _	8 - 7 = _	8 - 8 = _	5 - 4 = _
2 - 1 = _	9 - 6 = _	5 - 5 = _	5 - 5 = _	2 - 1 = _
2 - 2 = _	8 - 2 = _	7 - 1 = _	7 - 4 = _	8 - 8 = _
4 - 2 = _	3 - 2 = _	5 - 4 = _	7 - 6 = _	9 - 6 = _
8 - 8 = _	5 - 3 = _	9 - 7 = _	9 - 2 = _	6 - 6 = _
6 - 4 = _	9 - 3 = _	7 - 2 = _	9 - 6 = _	7 - 4 = _
9 - 3 = _	9 - 2 = _	5 - 2 = _	9 - 5 = _	4 - 4 = _
9 - 2 = _	6 - 6 = _	10 - 9 = _	8 - 3 = _	7 - 2 = _

S

9 - 7 = _	8 - 5 = _	8 - 6 = _	7 - 7 = _	6 - 3 = _
9 - 6 = _	5 - 3 = _	4 - 2 = _	7 - 4 = _	6 - 6 = _
5 - 2 = _	9 - 8 = _	7 - 2 = _	6 - 6 = _	9 - 7 = _
8 - 7 = _	9 - 5 = _	5 - 4 = _	10 - 3 = _	3 - 2 = _
10 - 4 = _	4 - 2 = _	7 - 7 = _	6 - 3 = _	9 - 2 = _
3 - 2 = _	8 - 6 = _	6 - 1 = _	2 - 2 = _	7 - 3 = _
2 - 1 = _	6 - 2 = _	10 - 1 = _	7 - 5 = _	10 - 4 = _
8 - 4 = _	3 - 2 = _	5 - 5 = _	10 - 3 = _	10 - 7 = _

T

9 - 3 = _	5 - 1 = _	8 - 2 = _	7 - 3 = _	7 - 5 = _
4 - 4 = _	10 - 5 = _	9 - 2 = _	3 - 1 = _	8 - 2 = _
8 - 6 = _	10 - 4 = _	6 - 2 = _	6 - 1 = _	8 - 7 = _
9 - 6 = _	7 - 2 = _	3 - 3 = _	5 - 2 = _	7 - 4 = _
7 - 4 = _	5 - 4 = _	8 - 4 = _	9 - 3 = _	7 - 2 = _
8 - 2 = _	3 - 1 = _	6 - 3 = _	9 - 2 = _	7 - 1 = _
7 - 3 = _	9 - 9 = _	10 - 4 = _	8 - 6 = _	7 - 6 = _
5 - 4 = _	9 - 2 = _	8 - 3 = _	4 - 3 = _	6 - 1 = _

U

9 - 8 = _	5 - 2 = _	7 - 3 = _	2 - 1 = _	5 - 1 = _
3 - 2 = _	10 - 2 = _	8 - 4 = _	8 - 4 = _	5 - 3 = _
3 - 3 = _	5 - 1 = _	6 - 2 = _	9 - 4 = _	9 - 8 = _
9 - 7 = _	7 - 4 = _	5 - 1 = _	10 - 9 = _	10 - 2 = _
5 - 4 = _	6 - 3 = _	10 - 1 = _	7 - 6 = _	8 - 6 = _
8 - 5 = _	9 - 4 = _	9 - 8 = _	7 - 4 = _	8 - 4 = _
9 - 2 = _	7 - 5 = _	8 - 2 = _	7 - 7 = _	9 - 6 = _
9 - 7 = _	2 - 1 = _	9 - 7 = _	10 - 3 = _	5 - 5 = _

V

9 - 2 = _	9 - 5 = _	9 - 2 = _	7 - 4 = _	8 - 7 = _
6 - 4 = _	7 - 3 = _	6 - 2 = _	9 - 6 = _	8 - 3 = _
6 - 2 = _	7 - 7 = _	3 - 2 = _	9 - 1 = _	5 - 1 = _
9 - 1 = _	6 - 2 = _	7 - 7 = _	9 - 4 = _	8 - 5 = _
9 - 3 = _	7 - 2 = _	8 - 2 = _	7 - 6 = _	2 - 2 = _
7 - 3 = _	8 - 4 = _	6 - 3 = _	5 - 3 = _	8 - 5 = _
4 - 2 = _	4 - 2 = _	9 - 1 = _	9 - 3 = _	9 - 9 = _
6 - 6 = _	8 - 4 = _	9 - 8 = _	4 - 3 = _	8 - 3 = _

Answer Key

A

2 + 4 = 6	4 + 2 = 6	7 + 2 = 9	6 + 3 = 9	4 + 1 = 5
5 + 3 = 8	5 + 2 = 7	2 + 1 = 3	3 + 4 = 7	2 + 7 = 9
5 + 4 = 9	2 + 5 = 7	5 + 2 = 7	1 + 4 = 5	4 + 5 = 9
1 + 4 = 5	7 + 2 = 9	2 + 5 = 7	3 + 2 = 5	2 + 7 = 9
5 + 3 = 8	3 + 6 = 9	5 + 1 = 6	7 + 3 = 10	4 + 2 = 6
3 + 7 = 10	1 + 9 = 10	3 + 2 = 5	2 + 5 = 7	4 + 5 = 9
2 + 7 = 9	2 + 3 = 5	4 + 5 = 9	3 + 7 = 10	1 + 5 = 6
4 + 3 = 7	2 + 4 = 6	4 + 2 = 6	1 + 8 = 9	8 + 2 = 10

B

8 + 2 = 10	7 + 3 = 10	3 + 3 = 6	7 + 3 = 10	5 + 5 = 10
2 + 6 = 8	2 + 8 = 10	1 + 2 = 3	8 + 2 = 10	5 + 5 = 10
6 + 1 = 7	3 + 2 = 5	5 + 4 = 9	3 + 3 = 6	3 + 3 = 6
4 + 3 = 7	4 + 5 = 9	3 + 3 = 6	7 + 1 = 8	6 + 4 = 10
2 + 7 = 9	4 + 2 = 6	5 + 5 = 10	8 + 2 = 10	5 + 2 = 7
1 + 8 = 9	2 + 6 = 8	1 + 1 = 2	2 + 2 = 4	5 + 5 = 10
2 + 7 = 9	5 + 3 = 8	7 + 3 = 10	8 + 1 = 9	1 + 7 = 8
5 + 2 = 7	3 + 7 = 10	2 + 5 = 7	3 + 4 = 7	2 + 4 = 6

C

2 + 3 = 5	4 + 6 = 10	3 + 3 = 6	2 + 5 = 7	2 + 5 = 7
2 + 2 = 4	5 + 4 = 9	3 + 3 = 6	1 + 3 = 4	3 + 4 = 7
1 + 3 = 4	2 + 3 = 5	3 + 6 = 9	3 + 2 = 5	3 + 7 = 10
3 + 6 = 9	8 + 1 = 9	4 + 3 = 7	6 + 2 = 8	9 + 1 = 10
4 + 4 = 8	5 + 4 = 9	1 + 9 = 10	3 + 4 = 7	4 + 2 = 6
3 + 6 = 9	7 + 2 = 9	1 + 8 = 9	7 + 1 = 8	9 + 1 = 10
4 + 2 = 6	2 + 6 = 8	2 + 3 = 5	2 + 7 = 9	1 + 3 = 4
5 + 4 = 9	4 + 3 = 7	2 + 1 = 3	3 + 6 = 9	2 + 7 = 9

D

3 + 2 = 5	7 + 2 = 9	2 + 2 = 4	4 + 3 = 7	2 + 8 = 10
6 + 4 = 10	2 + 6 = 8	5 + 3 = 8	4 + 3 = 7	4 + 6 = 10
8 + 2 = 10	2 + 3 = 5	2 + 3 = 5	7 + 3 = 10	3 + 7 = 10
4 + 4 = 8	1 + 7 = 8	1 + 2 = 3	3 + 3 = 6	1 + 5 = 6
1 + 7 = 8	2 + 5 = 7	7 + 3 = 10	2 + 5 = 7	9 + 1 = 10
2 + 3 = 5	2 + 6 = 8	2 + 2 = 4	3 + 4 = 7	6 + 3 = 9
7 + 1 = 8	5 + 4 = 9	3 + 5 = 8	9 + 1 = 10	6 + 2 = 8
1 + 2 = 3	1 + 5 = 6	2 + 8 = 10	4 + 1 = 5	3 + 5 = 8

E

4 + 3 = 7   3 + 4 = 7   2 + 5 = 7   5 + 5 = 10   6 + 2 = 8

6 + 4 = 10   1 + 1 = 2   4 + 2 = 6   7 + 2 = 9   2 + 2 = 4

3 + 5 = 8   6 + 3 = 9   1 + 5 = 6   6 + 4 = 10   5 + 2 = 7

4 + 5 = 9   3 + 4 = 7   2 + 8 = 10   6 + 3 = 9   3 + 6 = 9

2 + 4 = 6   7 + 2 = 9   7 + 1 = 8   1 + 2 = 3   1 + 8 = 9

3 + 6 = 9   2 + 6 = 8   5 + 3 = 8   6 + 4 = 10   2 + 7 = 9

3 + 3 = 6   3 + 3 = 6   7 + 2 = 9   2 + 3 = 5   3 + 6 = 9

2 + 8 = 10   3 + 7 = 10   1 + 2 = 3   3 + 7 = 10   2 + 2 = 4

F

2 + 8 = 10   3 + 7 = 10   5 + 3 = 8   2 + 5 = 7   6 + 2 = 8

4 + 2 = 6   1 + 8 = 9   2 + 6 = 8   1 + 4 = 5   3 + 5 = 8

1 + 4 = 5   2 + 5 = 7   3 + 2 = 5   3 + 5 = 8   7 + 3 = 10

2 + 3 = 5   7 + 2 = 9   5 + 3 = 8   1 + 5 = 6   2 + 8 = 10

2 + 3 = 5   3 + 2 = 5   4 + 4 = 8   4 + 5 = 9   5 + 1 = 6

5 + 5 = 10   6 + 4 = 10   5 + 2 = 7   5 + 4 = 9   3 + 6 = 9

2 + 1 = 3   5 + 5 = 10   6 + 4 = 10   2 + 8 = 10   3 + 5 = 8

3 + 6 = 9   6 + 1 = 7   6 + 2 = 8   8 + 2 = 10   4 + 1 = 5

G

+ 2 = 7   8 + 1 = 9   2 + 5 = 7   1 + 9 = 10   4 + 3 = 7

+ 3 = 5   4 + 2 = 6   4 + 5 = 9   3 + 5 = 8   7 + 2 = 9

+ 7 = 10   3 + 7 = 10   1 + 9 = 10   6 + 2 = 8   4 + 4 = 8

+ 7 = 10   8 + 2 = 10   3 + 4 = 7   6 + 3 = 9   7 + 1 = 8

+ 6 = 8   2 + 5 = 7   4 + 3 = 7   3 + 7 = 10   2 + 6 = 8

+ 6 = 10   3 + 6 = 9   5 + 4 = 9   6 + 2 = 8   3 + 1 = 4

+ 6 = 10   5 + 1 = 6   4 + 6 = 10   7 + 1 = 8   4 + 6 = 10

+ 1 = 5   4 + 1 = 5   7 + 2 = 9   5 + 2 = 7   2 + 8 = 10

H

9 + 1 = 10   5 + 5 = 10   4 + 4 = 8   8 + 2 = 10   1 + 9 = 10

5 + 5 = 10   1 + 7 = 8   6 + 2 = 8   3 + 7 = 10   2 + 3 = 5

2 + 6 = 8   3 + 3 = 6   2 + 4 = 6   3 + 3 = 6   1 + 5 = 6

2 + 6 = 8   5 + 3 = 8   1 + 9 = 10   1 + 8 = 9   3 + 7 = 10

3 + 7 = 10   7 + 2 = 9   4 + 1 = 5   2 + 7 = 9   6 + 3 = 9

2 + 1 = 3   6 + 2 = 8   5 + 5 = 10   4 + 3 = 7   3 + 5 = 8

1 + 8 = 9   4 + 3 = 7   4 + 3 = 7   5 + 5 = 10   1 + 8 = 9

2 + 8 = 10   7 + 2 = 9   4 + 1 = 5   6 + 2 = 8   6 + 3 = 9

I

3 + 6 = 9	7 + 1 = 8	1 + 9 = 10	2 + 4 = 6	6 + 4 = 10
5 + 3 = 8	7 + 3 = 10	6 + 2 = 8	3 + 5 = 8	6 + 4 = 10
1 + 8 = 9	4 + 1 = 5	2 + 3 = 5	6 + 3 = 9	8 + 1 = 9
3 + 7 = 10	4 + 2 = 6	3 + 5 = 8	6 + 4 = 10	2 + 3 = 5
8 + 1 = 9	4 + 5 = 9	6 + 2 = 8	1 + 4 = 5	3 + 7 = 10
6 + 4 = 10	4 + 4 = 8	9 + 1 = 10	7 + 2 = 9	5 + 2 = 7
3 + 7 = 10	3 + 6 = 9	3 + 7 = 10	3 + 7 = 10	2 + 3 = 5
2 + 2 = 4	1 + 3 = 4	4 + 3 = 7	7 + 2 = 9	2 + 1 = 3

J

3 + 6 = 9	8 + 2 = 10	5 + 4 = 9	1 + 2 = 3	3 + 1 = 4
4 + 2 = 6	3 + 3 = 6	4 + 4 = 8	3 + 1 = 4	1 + 2 = 3
3 + 7 = 10	3 + 3 = 6	3 + 4 = 7	2 + 4 = 6	7 + 3 = 10
1 + 9 = 10	1 + 1 = 2	1 + 4 = 5	5 + 4 = 9	3 + 1 = 4
8 + 2 = 10	5 + 4 = 9	1 + 5 = 6	1 + 4 = 5	2 + 6 = 8
5 + 2 = 7	6 + 1 = 7	3 + 7 = 10	1 + 3 = 4	1 + 4 = 5
4 + 3 = 7	6 + 3 = 9	4 + 4 = 8	4 + 5 = 9	3 + 4 = 7
2 + 4 = 6	2 + 5 = 7	6 + 3 = 9	1 + 3 = 4	5 + 3 = 8

K

1 + 9 = 10	2 + 3 = 5	5 + 4 = 9	2 + 1 = 3	8 + 2 = 10
2 + 4 = 6	2 + 8 = 10	6 + 3 = 9	2 + 6 = 8	7 + 2 = 9
6 + 2 = 8	2 + 8 = 10	2 + 2 = 4	2 + 8 = 10	6 + 3 = 9
2 + 4 = 6	3 + 2 = 5	2 + 5 = 7	8 + 2 = 10	2 + 3 = 5
1 + 3 = 4	6 + 2 = 8	2 + 6 = 8	1 + 3 = 4	3 + 2 = 5
5 + 2 = 7	3 + 3 = 6	1 + 3 = 4	2 + 7 = 9	3 + 7 = 10
6 + 2 = 8	2 + 1 = 3	4 + 1 = 5	3 + 6 = 9	3 + 7 = 10
4 + 2 = 6	9 + 1 = 10	5 + 3 = 8	3 + 4 = 7	1 + 9 = 10

L

5 - 5 = 0	10 - 6 = 4	8 - 1 = 7	5 - 5 = 0	7 - 7 = 0
8 - 4 = 4	7 - 6 = 1	10 - 9 = 1	5 - 2 = 3	9 - 9 = 0
8 - 4 = 4	7 - 3 = 4	9 - 7 = 2	6 - 4 = 2	6 - 6 = 0
7 - 5 = 2	8 - 2 = 6	9 - 3 = 6	6 - 4 = 2	3 - 2 = 1
8 - 7 = 1	9 - 8 = 1	7 - 2 = 5	5 - 3 = 2	6 - 5 = 1
8 - 5 = 3	8 - 2 = 6	8 - 4 = 4	3 - 3 = 0	9 - 6 = 3
9 - 8 = 1	9 - 3 = 6	9 - 8 = 1	10 - 4 = 6	7 - 6 = 1
9 - 6 = 3	8 - 6 = 2	8 - 8 = 0	8 - 7 = 1	9 - 3 = 6

M

8 - 7 = 1 4 - 1 = 3 9 - 1 = 8 9 - 6 = 3 9 - 2 = 7

6 - 1 = 5 8 - 7 = 1 9 - 6 = 3 8 - 4 = 4 8 - 3 = 5

9 - 8 = 1 8 - 3 = 5 10 - 1 = 9 8 - 5 = 3 6 - 2 = 4

9 - 1 = 8 5 - 3 = 2 10 - 8 = 2 7 - 3 = 4 7 - 6 = 1

9 - 2 = 7 4 - 2 = 2 9 - 7 = 2 8 - 5 = 3 9 - 5 = 4

8 - 8 = 0 6 - 4 = 2 4 - 2 = 2 2 - 2 = 0 3 - 2 = 1

10 - 1 = 9 7 - 3 = 4 9 - 5 = 4 9 - 1 = 8 3 - 2 = 1

4 - 3 = 1 6 - 6 = 0 6 - 2 = 4 9 - 2 = 7 9 - 6 = 3

N

9 - 6 = 3 5 - 2 = 3 8 - 4 = 4 4 - 4 = 0 3 - 2 = 1

10 - 4 = 6 9 - 4 = 5 8 - 4 = 4 6 - 1 = 5 6 - 5 = 1

9 - 4 = 5 5 - 1 = 4 10 - 9 = 1 2 - 2 = 0 7 - 1 = 6

10 - 8 = 2 8 - 5 = 3 9 - 4 = 5 6 - 1 = 5 10 - 9 = 1

4 - 4 = 0 6 - 6 = 0 10 - 3 = 7 1 - 1 = 0 8 - 6 = 2

8 - 3 = 5 6 - 5 = 1 7 - 3 = 4 7 - 3 = 4 7 - 7 = 0

4 - 2 = 2 4 - 3 = 1 9 - 4 = 5 7 - 2 = 5 8 - 7 = 1

10 - 7 = 3 9 - 2 = 7 5 - 3 = 2 2 - 1 = 1 10 - 8 = 2

O

6 - 4 = 2 2 - 1 = 1 5 - 3 = 2 6 - 2 = 4 10 - 8 = 2

6 - 5 = 1 9 - 2 = 7 6 - 3 = 3 6 - 5 = 1 5 - 4 = 1

9 - 5 = 4 8 - 5 = 3 4 - 2 = 2 2 - 2 = 0 6 - 1 = 5

6 - 4 = 2 9 - 9 = 0 6 - 2 = 4 10 - 2 = 8 9 - 1 = 8

3 - 2 = 1 8 - 4 = 4 10 - 4 = 6 10 - 4 = 6 8 - 5 = 3

5 - 2 = 3 4 - 3 = 1 9 - 7 = 2 3 - 2 = 1 5 - 3 = 2

6 - 5 = 1 8 - 4 = 4 8 - 3 = 5 8 - 7 = 1 4 - 3 = 1

8 - 6 = 2 8 - 2 = 6 8 - 3 = 5 5 - 3 = 2 8 - 5 = 3

P

5 - 5 = 0 6 - 4 = 2 10 - 8 = 2 4 - 4 = 0 9 - 5 = 4

10 - 5 = 5 3 - 2 = 1 8 - 4 = 4 6 - 4 = 2 9 - 2 = 7

4 - 4 = 0 6 - 5 = 1 7 - 3 = 4 5 - 4 = 1 1 - 1 = 0

5 - 4 = 1 5 - 5 = 0 8 - 1 = 7 4 - 2 = 2 9 - 7 = 2

7 - 4 = 3 4 - 1 = 3 8 - 5 = 3 9 - 6 = 3 9 - 3 = 6

9 - 8 = 1 6 - 5 = 1 8 - 5 = 3 7 - 4 = 3 8 - 3 = 5

9 - 1 = 8 7 - 3 = 4 9 - 8 = 1 9 - 2 = 7 2 - 1 = 1

9 - 1 = 8 9 - 8 = 1 9 - 4 = 5 9 - 5 = 4 8 - 4 = 4

Q

8 - 3 = 5	5 - 5 = 0	4 - 2 = 2	9 - 9 = 0	6 - 2 = 4
9 - 4 = 5	8 - 3 = 5	9 - 6 = 3	6 - 2 = 4	6 - 2 = 4
6 - 5 = 1	7 - 1 = 6	7 - 5 = 2	4 - 3 = 1	5 - 1 = 4
6 - 5 = 1	7 - 3 = 4	9 - 7 = 2	10 - 6 = 4	8 - 4 = 4
2 - 1 = 1	9 - 4 = 5	5 - 5 = 0	5 - 3 = 2	7 - 5 = 2
6 - 3 = 3	9 - 3 = 6	5 - 1 = 4	8 - 2 = 6	6 - 3 = 3
7 - 2 = 5	10 - 9 = 1	8 - 4 = 4	7 - 6 = 1	4 - 3 = 1
6 - 4 = 2	9 - 2 = 7	6 - 6 = 0	9 - 2 = 7	6 - 5 = 1

R

8 - 2 = 6	7 - 4 = 3	8 - 7 = 1	8 - 8 = 0	5 - 4 = 1
2 - 1 = 1	9 - 6 = 3	5 - 5 = 0	5 - 5 = 0	2 - 1 = 1
2 - 2 = 0	8 - 2 = 6	7 - 1 = 6	7 - 4 = 3	8 - 8 = 0
4 - 2 = 2	3 - 2 = 1	5 - 4 = 1	7 - 6 = 1	9 - 6 = 3
8 - 8 = 0	5 - 3 = 2	9 - 7 = 2	9 - 2 = 7	6 - 6 = 0
6 - 4 = 2	9 - 3 = 6	7 - 2 = 5	9 - 6 = 3	7 - 4 = 3
9 - 3 = 6	9 - 2 = 7	5 - 2 = 3	9 - 5 = 4	4 - 4 = 0
9 - 2 = 7	6 - 6 = 0	10 - 9 = 1	8 - 3 = 5	7 - 2 = 5

S

9 - 7 = 2	8 - 5 = 3	8 - 6 = 2	7 - 7 = 0	6 - 3 = 3
9 - 6 = 3	5 - 3 = 2	4 - 2 = 2	7 - 4 = 3	6 - 6 = 0
5 - 2 = 3	9 - 8 = 1	7 - 2 = 5	6 - 6 = 0	9 - 7 = 2
8 - 7 = 1	9 - 5 = 4	5 - 4 = 1	10 - 3 = 7	3 - 2 = 1
10 - 4 = 6	4 - 2 = 2	7 - 7 = 0	6 - 3 = 3	9 - 2 = 7
3 - 2 = 1	8 - 6 = 2	6 - 1 = 5	2 - 2 = 0	7 - 3 = 4
2 - 1 = 1	6 - 2 = 4	10 - 1 = 9	7 - 5 = 2	10 - 4 = 6
8 - 4 = 4	3 - 2 = 1	5 - 5 = 0	10 - 3 = 7	10 - 7 = 3

T

9 - 3 = 6	5 - 1 = 4	8 - 2 = 6	7 - 3 = 4	7 - 5 = 2
4 - 4 = 0	10 - 5 = 5	9 - 2 = 7	3 - 1 = 2	8 - 2 = 6
8 - 6 = 2	10 - 4 = 6	6 - 2 = 4	6 - 1 = 5	8 - 7 = 1
9 - 6 = 3	7 - 2 = 5	3 - 3 = 0	5 - 2 = 3	7 - 4 = 3
7 - 4 = 3	5 - 4 = 1	8 - 4 = 4	9 - 3 = 6	7 - 2 = 5
8 - 2 = 6	3 - 1 = 2	6 - 3 = 3	9 - 2 = 7	7 - 1 = 6
7 - 3 = 4	9 - 9 = 0	10 - 4 = 6	8 - 6 = 2	7 - 6 = 1
5 - 4 = 1	9 - 2 = 7	8 - 3 = 5	4 - 3 = 1	6 - 1 = 5

U

8 = 1	5 - 2 = 3	7 - 3 = 4	2 - 1 = 1	5 - 1 = 4
2 = 1	10 - 2 = 8	8 - 4 = 4	8 - 4 = 4	5 - 3 = 2
3 = 0	5 - 1 = 4	6 - 2 = 4	9 - 4 = 5	9 - 8 = 1
7 = 2	7 - 4 = 3	5 - 1 = 4	10 - 9 = 1	10 - 2 = 8
4 = 1	6 - 3 = 3	10 - 1 = 9	7 - 6 = 1	8 - 6 = 2
5 = 3	9 - 4 = 5	9 - 8 = 1	7 - 4 = 3	8 - 4 = 4
2 = 7	7 - 5 = 2	8 - 2 = 6	7 - 7 = 0	9 - 6 = 3
7 = 2	2 - 1 = 1	9 - 7 = 2	10 - 3 = 7	5 - 5 = 0

V

9 - 2 = 7	9 - 5 = 4	9 - 2 = 7	7 - 4 = 3	8 - 7 = 1
6 - 4 = 2	7 - 3 = 4	6 - 2 = 4	9 - 6 = 3	8 - 3 = 5
6 - 2 = 4	7 - 7 = 0	3 - 2 = 1	9 - 1 = 8	5 - 1 = 4
9 - 1 = 8	6 - 2 = 4	7 - 7 = 0	9 - 4 = 5	8 - 5 = 3
9 - 3 = 6	7 - 2 = 5	8 - 2 = 6	7 - 6 = 1	2 - 2 = 0
7 - 3 = 4	8 - 4 = 4	6 - 3 = 3	5 - 3 = 2	8 - 5 = 3
4 - 2 = 2	4 - 2 = 2	9 - 1 = 8	9 - 3 = 6	9 - 9 = 0
6 - 6 = 0	8 - 4 = 4	9 - 8 = 1	4 - 3 = 1	8 - 3 = 5

Dear Parents, Guardians, and Educators,

Our only hope is that this book helped your child in anyway better his/her ability in getting started with mathematics.

Would you mind taking the time to leaving a review on the website you bought this from? It would be very much appreciated!

Have a wonderful day,

Jaime Patterson

Made in the USA
Monee, IL
07 July 2026

56685307R00037